EXECUTIVE SUMMARY

Malaysia is a federal constitutional monarchy. It has a parliamentary system of government selected through regular, multiparty elections and is headed by a prime minister. The king is the head of state and serves a largely ceremonial role; he serves a five-year term, and the kingship rotates among the sultans of the nine states with hereditary rulers. The United Malays National Organization (UMNO), together with a coalition of political parties known as the National Front (BN), has held power since independence in 1957. In the 2013 general election, the BN lost the popular vote to the opposition coalition but was re-elected in the country's first-past-the-post system. The opposition and civil society organizations alleged electoral irregularities and systemic disadvantages for opposition groups due to lack of media access and gerrymandered districts favoring the ruling coalition.

Civilian authorities at times did not maintain effective control over security forces.

The most significant human rights problems included government restrictions on freedoms of speech and expression, press and media, assembly, and association. In the wake of a government financial scandal dating back to 2014, whistleblowers and critics faced censorship, police intimidation, investigation, and criminal charges. Print and broadcast media outlets self-censored news coverage of the scandal. Online media offered more independent and critical perspectives, but were often the target of legal action and harassment, leading one site to shut down. Restrictions on freedom of religion were also a significant concern--including bans on religious groups, restrictions on proselytizing, and prohibitions on the freedom to change one's religion.

Other human rights problems included deaths during police apprehension and while in custody; laws allowing detention without trial; caning as a form of punishment imposed by criminal and "sharia" (Islamic law) courts; restrictions on the rights of migrants, including migrant workers, refugees, and victims of human trafficking; official corruption; violence and discrimination against women; and discrimination against lesbian, gay, bisexual, transgender, and intersex persons. Longstanding government policies gave preference to ethnic Malays in many areas. The government restricted union and collective-bargaining activity, and government policies created vulnerabilities for child labor and forced labor problems, especially for migrant workers.

The government arrested and prosecuted some officials engaged in corruption, malfeasance, and human rights abuses, although civil society groups alleged continued impunity.

Section 1. Respect for the Integrity of the Person, Including Freedom from:

a. Arbitrary Deprivation of Life and other Unlawful or Politically Motivated Killings

There were reports the government or its agents committed arbitrary or unlawful killings. In June the government disclosed there were 50 deaths in police custody from the beginning of 2013 through April, with only one death allegedly caused by the police. Civil society activists disputed this, claiming police were responsible for more of the deaths in custody.

In April a government commission found police culpable for the 2013 death of N. Dharmendran, and detailed efforts by police to cover up the case and alter evidence. In June a court acquitted the four police officers charged with the murder. Human rights organizations criticized the decision, and noted the rarity of successful prosecutions in death-in-custody cases.

b. Disappearance

There were no reports of politically motivated disappearances.

c. Torture and Other Cruel, Inhuman, or Degrading Treatment or Punishment

No law specifically prohibits torture; however, laws that prohibit "committing grievous hurt" encompass torture. More than 60 offenses are subject to caning, and judges routinely mandated caning in response to crimes including kidnapping, rape, robbery, narcotics possession, criminal breach of trust, migrant smuggling, and immigration offenses.

Civil and criminal law exempt men older than 50 years, unless convicted of rape, and all women from caning. Male children between 10 and 18 years may receive a maximum of 10 strokes of a "light cane" in a public courtroom. The government revealed in a letter to a member of parliament that authorities caned 8,451 prisoners (5,968 foreigners and 2,483 citizens) in 2013.

Some states' sharia laws--those governing family issues and certain crimes under Islam and that apply to all Muslims--also prescribe caning for certain offenses. Women are not exempt from caning under sharia, and national courts have not resolved issues involving conflicts among the constitution, the penal code, and sharia.

In January a human rights nongovernmental organization (NGO) released handwritten accounts by seven suspected terrorists held under investigatory detention alleging maltreatment, including beatings, sexual humiliation, and forced confessions. In July, R. Sri Sanjeevan, an activist working on police corruption and whom police arrested on extortion charges, said police blindfolded and beat him while denying him medical treatment.

Prison and Detention Center Conditions

Conditions in prisons and detention centers operated by the government's Immigration Department were harsh.

Physical Conditions: Overcrowding in prisons and immigration detention centers, particularly in facilities near major cities, remained a serious problem.

Some prisoners and detainees died, including while in police holding cells. In May the government revealed that from the beginning of 2013 through April, 721 prisoners died in the country's prisons, an average of 18 deaths per month. International media reported allegations of deaths in immigration detention centers, but official statistics were not available.

Administration: Authorities used caning in combination with imprisonment for some nonviolent offenders. Prisoners and detainees had freedom of religious observance provided religious practices did not derive from one of the sects of Islam the government bans as "deviant." The law does not provide a process for prisoners to submit complaints to judicial authorities, but it allows judges to visit prisons to examine conditions and ask prisoners and prison officials about prison conditions. Authorities generally treated attorney-client communications as private and confidential.

Independent Monitoring: Authorities generally did not permit NGOs and media to monitor prison conditions. The government provided regular prison access to the International Committee of the Red Cross (ICRC) and SUHAKAM, the government human rights commission, on a case-by-case basis. In 2015 the ICRC conducted 27 visits to seven prisons, seven immigration detention centers, and one temporary detention center, visiting 24,845 detainees.

The Office of the UN High Commissioner for Refugees (UNHCR) generally had access to registered refugees, asylum seekers, and unregistered persons of concern who may have claims to asylum and refugee status and who authorities held in immigration detention centers and prisons. This access, however, was not always timely.

d. Arbitrary Arrest or Detention

Police may detain persons suspected of terrorism, organized crime, gang activity, and trafficking in drugs or persons without a warrant or judicial review for two-year terms, renewable indefinitely. Within seven days of the initial detention, however, police must present the case for detention to a public prosecutor. If the prosecutor agrees "sufficient evidence exists to justify" continued detention and further investigation, a fact-finding inquiry officer appointed by the minister of home affairs must report within 59 days to a detention board appointed by the king. The board may renew the detention order or impose an order to restrict--without trial or judicial review--a suspect's place of residence, travel, access to communications facilities, and use of the internet for a maximum of five years. Details on the numbers of those detained or under restriction orders were not generally available.

The law allows investigative detention to prevent a criminal suspect from fleeing or destroying evidence during an investigation. Immigration law allows authorities to arrest and detain noncitizens for 30 days pending a deportation decision.

Some observers criticized other legal provisions that allow the identity of witnesses to be kept secret (inhibiting cross-examination of witnesses) and allow authorities to detain the accused after an acquittal in case the prosecution decides to appeal.

Investigation into use of deadly force by a police officer occurs only if the attorney general initiates the investigation or if he approves an application for an investigation by family members of the deceased. When the attorney general orders an official inquiry, a coroner's court convenes, and the hearing is open to the public. In such cases the court generally issues an open verdict, which means there was no verdict and it would take no further action against police.

Role of the Police and Security Apparatus

The Royal Malaysia Police force, with approximately 102,000 members, reports to the home affairs minister. The inspector general of police is responsible for organizing and administering the police force. The Ministry of Home Affairs also oversees immigration and border enforcement. State-level Islamic religious enforcement officers have authority to accompany police on raids or conduct their own raids of private premises and public establishments to enforce sharia, including bans on indecent dress, alcohol consumption, sale of restricted books, or close proximity to members of the opposite sex. Religious authorities at the state level administer sharia for civil and family law through Islamic courts and have jurisdiction for all Muslims. The Ministry of Home Affairs also oversees the People's Volunteer Corps (RELA), a paramilitary civilian volunteer corps. NGOs remained concerned inadequate training left RELA members poorly equipped to perform their duties.

The government has some mechanisms to investigate and punish abuse and corruption, and SUHAKAM played a role in investigating alleged abuses committed by the security forces. NGOs and media reported that despite investigation into some incidents, security forces often acted with impunity.

Police officers are subject to trial by criminal and civil courts. Police representatives reported there were disciplinary actions against police officers, and punishments included suspension, dismissal, and demotion. Civil society groups and NGOs continued to call for establishment of an independent police complaints and misconduct commission. Government officials and police opposed the idea. Police training included human rights awareness in its courses. SUHAKAM also conducted human rights training and workshops for police and prison officials.

Arrest Procedures and Treatment of Detainees

The law permits police to arrest and detain individuals for some offenses without a warrant. Although police generally observed legal provisions regarding arrest, NGOs reported the police practice of releasing suspects and then quickly re-arresting and holding them in continued investigative custody. Some NGOs asserted a police approach of "arrest first, investigate later" was prevalent, particularly in cases involving allegations of terrorism. By law an arrested person has the right to be informed of the grounds for arrest by the arresting police officer. To facilitate investigations police can remand an arrested person for 24 hours, which can be extended for up to 14 days by a court order under general criminal law provisions.

In June police arrested and re-arrested activist and police critic R. Sri Sanjeevan eight times during a two-month period under different allegations before finally detaining him under an anti-organized crime provision that allows for a 21-day detention period. He successfully challenged his remand order in court, and authorities freed him a few days later.

Bail is usually available for persons accused of crimes not punishable by life imprisonment or death. The amount and availability of bail is at the judge's discretion. Persons granted bail usually must surrender their passports to the court.

Police must inform detainees of the right to contact family members and consult a lawyer of their choice. Nonetheless, police often denied detainees access to legal counsel and questioned suspects without allowing a lawyer to be present. Police justified this practice as necessary to prevent interference in investigations in progress, and the courts generally upheld the practice. On occasion police did not allow prompt access to family members.

The law allows the detention of a material witness in a criminal case if that person is likely to flee.

Arbitrary Arrest: Authorities sometimes used their powers to intimidate and punish opponents of the government. In April police arrested and charged opposition Member of Parliament Rafizi Ramli with leaking state secrets after he released part of an audit report he claimed linked a continued government financial scandal to late payments to military veterans. Human rights organizations and the political opposition criticized the arrest as breaching parliamentary privileges and intimidating other elected representatives to silence. In November authorities sentenced Rafizi to 18 months in prison, although he remained free pending an appeal. Unless the sentence is overturned or reduced to less than 12 months, Rafizi will be disqualified from seeking re-election.

Pretrial Detention: Crowded and understaffed courts often resulted in lengthy pretrial detention, sometimes lasting several years. The International Center for Prison Studies reported that pretrial detainees made up approximately 26 percent of the prisoner population as of mid-2015.

Detainee's Ability to Challenge Lawfulness of Detention before a Court: Detainees have the right to challenge their detention by filing a habeas corpus application. In July a lower court freed anticorruption campaigner R. Sri

Sanjeevan, declaring his remand under an anti-organized crime law null and void.

e. Denial of Fair Public Trial

Three constitutional articles provide the basis for an independent judiciary; however, other constitutional provisions, legislation restricting judicial review, and additional factors limited judicial independence and strengthened executive influence over the judiciary.

Members of the bar, NGO representatives, and other observers expressed serious concern about significant limitations on judicial independence, citing a number of high-profile instances of arbitrary verdicts, selective prosecution, and preferential treatment of some litigants and lawyers.

In June, NGOs criticized the attorney general's decision to lead the prosecution of opposition leader and Penang State Chief Minister Lim Guan Eng, claiming a conflict of interest between the attorney-general's role as legal adviser to the government and a public prosecutor would create the perception of a politically motivated trial.

Trial Procedures

English common law is the basis for the civil legal system. The constitution states all persons are equal before the law and entitled to equal protection under the law. The law allows defendants a presumption of innocence until proven guilty. Judges conduct trials and render verdicts. Trials are public, although judges may order restrictions on press coverage. Defendants have the right to counsel at public expense if they face charges that carry the death penalty and may apply for a public defender in certain other cases.

According to the Malaysian Bar Council, defendants generally have adequate time and facilities to prepare a defense if they have the means to engage private counsel. Otherwise, defendants must rely on legal aid and the amount of time to prepare for trial is at the discretion of the judge. Authorities provide defendants free interpretation in Malay, Mandarin, Tamil, and some other commonly used dialects from the moment charged through all appeals. Strict rules of evidence apply in court; however, the government did not consistently make evidence available to defense counsel.

Defendants have the right to be present at their own trial, to confront witnesses against them, and present witnesses and evidence on their behalf, although judges sometimes disallowed witness testimony. Defendants may make statements for the record to an investigative agency prior to trial. Limited pretrial discovery in criminal cases impeded defendants' ability to defend themselves. Attorneys must apply for a court order to obtain documents covered under the official secrecy laws.

Defendants may appeal court decisions to higher courts, but only if the appeal raises a question of law or if material circumstances raise a reasonable doubt regarding conviction or sentencing. The Bar Council claimed these restrictions were excessive.

Many NGOs complained women did not receive fair treatment from sharia courts, especially in cases of divorce and child custody (see section 6).

Political Prisoners and Detainees

Opposition leader Anwar Ibrahim remained in prison, serving a five-year sentence for consensual sodomy, a charge many international observers and human rights organizations viewed as politically motivated. In December the federal court rejected his appeal to set aside his conviction and sentence.

Civil Judicial Procedures and Remedies

Individuals or organizations may sue the government and officials in court for alleged violations of human rights. The structure of the civil judiciary mirrors that of the criminal courts. A large case backlog often resulted in delayed court-ordered relief for civil plaintiffs. The courts have increasingly encouraged the use of mediation and arbitration to speed settlements.

f. Arbitrary or Unlawful Interference with Privacy, Family, Home, or Correspondence

Laws prohibit arbitrary interference with privacy rights; nevertheless, authorities sometimes infringed on citizens' privacy rights. Certain provisions allow police to enter and search without a warrant the homes of persons suspected of threatening national security. Police also may confiscate evidence under these provisions. Police used this legal authority to search homes and offices; seize computers, books, and newspapers; monitor conversations; and take persons into custody without a warrant. The government monitored the internet and threatened to detain anyone sending or posting content the government deemed a threat to public order or security (see section 2.a.).

Islamic authorities may enter private premises without a warrant if they deem swift action necessary to catch Muslims suspected of engaging in offenses such as gambling, consumption of alcohol, and sexual relations outside marriage.

The government bans membership in unregistered political parties and organizations.

The government does not recognize marriages between Muslims and non-Muslims and considers children born of such unions illegitimate.

Section 2. Respect for Civil Liberties, Including:

a. Freedom of Speech and Press

The constitution provides for freedom of speech and press, although it also provides for restrictions "in the interest of the security of the Federation…[or] public order." The government regularly enforced restrictions on freedom of expression by media, citing upholding Islam and the special status of ethnic Malays, protection of national security, public order, and friendly relations with other countries as reasons.

Freedom of Speech and Expression: The law prohibits sedition and public comment on issues defined as sensitive, including racial and religious matters or criticism of the king or ruling sultans. Sedition charges often stemmed from comments by vocal civil society or opposition leaders. Civil society groups claimed the government generally failed to investigate and prosecute similar "seditious" statements made by progovernment or pro-Malay persons.

In August judicial authorities sentenced an opposition leader to eight months in prison for a 2015 speech in which he called for the release of Anwar Ibrahim while suggesting politicians controlled the judiciary. The case was pending an appeal. Also in August a court found the president of a pro-Malay NGO guilty of sedition and fined him 2,000 Malaysian ringgit (RM) ($450) for an article he wrote calling the country's ethnic Chinese citizens "intruders."

Press and Media Freedoms: Political parties and individuals linked to the ruling coalition owned or controlled a majority of shares in almost all print and broadcast media, many of which were actively progovernment in their reporting. Online media outlets were more independent in their ownership and reporting but were often the target of legal action and harassment.

The government exerted control over news content, both in print and broadcast media; punished publishers of "malicious news," and banned, restricted, or limited circulation of publications believed a threat to public order, morality, or national security. The government has the power to suspend publication for these reasons, and retained effective control over the licensing process. In February the government blocked popular online news outlet *The Malaysian Insider* for "violating national laws," allegedly related to its reporting on a government financial scandal. The site closed a month later.

Authorities sometimes barred online media from covering government press conferences.

<u>Violence and Harassment</u>: Journalists were subject to harassment and intimidation due to their reporting. In April online news portal *Malaysiakini* recalled its journalist from covering state elections in Sarawak after she received online threats over an article she wrote reporting an elected official urged voters to choose the ruling coalition to ensure a Muslim continued to lead the religiously diverse state. Critics also lodged multiple police reports against the reporter and circulated her photo on social media, leading to concerns for her safety. In November a group of progovernment "Red Shirts" protesters gathered in front of *Malaysiakini's* offices and threatened to "tear down parts of the building."

<u>Censorship or Content Restrictions</u>: The government censored media, primarily print and broadcast media. In addition to controlling news content by banning or restricting publications believed to threaten public order, morality, or national security, the government prosecuted journalists for "malicious news," took little or no action against persons or organizations that abused journalists, and limited circulation of some publications. The law requires a permit to own a printing press, and printers often were reluctant to print publications critical of the government due to fear of reprisal. The government refused to issue printing permits to some online media outlets that were critical of the government. Such policies, together with antidefamation laws, inhibited independent or investigative journalism and resulted in extensive self-censorship in the print and broadcast media.

Despite these restrictions publications of opposition parties, social action groups, unions, internet news sites, and other private groups actively covered opposition parties and frequently printed views critical of government policies. Online media and blogs provided views and reported stories not featured in the mainstream press.

The government occasionally censored foreign magazines, foreign newspapers, and foreign-sourced television programming, most often due to sexual content.

The government's restrictions on radio and television stations mirrored those on print media, and all also predominantly supported the government. News about the opposition in those fora remained restricted and biased. Television stations censored programming to follow government guidelines.

The government generally restricted remarks or publications, including books, it judged might incite racial or religious disharmony. The Ministry of Home Affairs maintained a list of 1,593 banned books. In September the government announced four new banned publications "prejudicial to public order," including a report on torture in Malaysian prisons and a book criticizing the influence of Islam in the government.

Libel/Slander Laws: The law includes sections on civil and criminal defamation. Criminal defamation is punishable by a maximum of two years in jail, a fine, or both. True statements can be considered defamatory if they contravene the public good. The government used these laws, along with provisions against sedition, to punish and suppress publication of material critical of government officials and policies.

National Security: Authorities frequently cited laws protecting national security to restrict media distribution of material critical of government policies and public officials. In January the government blocked access to publishing platform *Medium* after it refused to remove an article hosted on its site about a financial corruption scandal involving the prime minister. The country's internet regulator claimed the article would "undermine Malaysia's social stability."

Nongovernmental Impact: Progovernment NGOs sought to limit freedom of expression through criminal complaints of allegedly seditious speech. Progovernment NGOs also sometimes attempted to intimidate opposition groups through demonstrations. In September police detained the leader of a progovernment NGO that threatened counterdemonstrations and physical violence against the leader of free and fair election NGO coalition Bersih, after Bersih announced a November mass protest against Prime Minister (PM) Najib Razak.

Internet Freedom

The government generally maintained a policy of open and free access to the internet, but authorities monitored the internet for e-mail messages and blog postings deemed a threat to public security or order.

The government warned internet users to avoid offensive or indecent content and sensitive matters such as religion and race, and aggressively pursued charges against those criticizing Islam or the country's royalty. In June a court sentenced a man to one year in prison after he pleaded guilty to insulting the Sultan of Johor on Facebook. In September an appeals court extended the man's sentence to three years, to be served in a "reform school."

Authorities also restricted internet freedom to combat dissenting views online. In January the government blocked two websites publishing documents alleging financial corruption at a state-owned development company, claiming the sites had published "false news," which threatened national security. Local and international human rights groups claimed the law does not allow the government to block websites unilaterally and it must instead seek a court finding.

Sedition and criminal defamation laws led to some self-censorship by local internet content sources such as bloggers, news providers, and NGO activists.

The law requires certain internet and other network service providers to obtain a license, and permits punishment of the owner of a website or blog for allowing offensive racial, religious, or political content. By regarding users who post content as publishers, the government places the burden of proof on the user in these cases. NGOs and members of the public criticized the law, noting it could cause self-censorship due to liability concerns.

According to the World Bank, approximately 17 million persons (67 percent of the population) had access to the internet.

Academic Freedom and Cultural Events

The government placed some restrictions on academic freedom, particularly the expression of unapproved political views, and enforced restrictions on teachers and students who expressed dissenting views. The government requires all civil servants, university faculty, and students to sign a pledge of loyalty to the king and government. Opposition leaders and human rights activists claimed the government used the loyalty pledge to restrain political activity among these groups.

Although faculty members sometimes publicly criticized the government, public university academics whose career advancement and funding depended on the government practiced self-censorship. Self-censorship took place among academics at private institutions as well, spurred by fears the government might revoke the licenses of their institutions. The law imposes limitations on student associations and on student and faculty political activity.

The government regularly censored films, editing out profanity, kissing, sex, and nudity. The government also censored films for certain political and religious content. The government did not allow cinemas to show films in Hebrew, Yiddish, or from Israel. Although the government allowed foreign films at local film festivals, it censored sexual content by blocking screens until the concerned scene was over. Media censorship rules forbid movies and songs that promote acceptance of gay persons (see section 6).

b. Freedom of Peaceful Assembly and Association

The constitution provides for the freedoms of assembly and association but allows restrictions deemed necessary or expedient in the interest of security, public order, or (in the case of association) morality. Abiding by the government's restrictions did not protect some protesters from harassment or arrest.

Freedom of Assembly

The constitution provides all citizens "the right to assemble peaceably and without arms;" however, several laws restricted this right. The law does not require groups to obtain a permit for assemblies. Nonetheless, police frequently placed time, location, and manner restrictions on the right to assemble. Authorities generally banned street protests, and police often confronted civil society and opposition demonstrations with water cannons, tear gas, and mass arrests. Protests deemed acceptable by the government usually proceeded without interference. In July police warned civil society coalition Bersih to avoid organizing protests that called for the resignation of PM Najib, later investigating Bersih and other civil society leaders for their roles in organizing an August protest.

Freedom of Association

The constitution provides for the right of association; however, the government placed significant restrictions on this right, and certain statutes limit it. By law only registered organizations of seven or more persons may legally function. The government often resisted registering organizations deemed particularly unfriendly to the government or imposed conditions when allowing a society to register. The government may revoke the registration of a society for violations of the law governing societies.

In September the government announced it would allow the provisional registration of a new political party formed by former members of the ruling coalition but placed restrictions on the party's name.

The law prohibits students who hold political posts from conducting political party activities on campus, and universities may ban any organization deemed "unsuitable to the interests and well-being of the students or the university." Students also are prohibited from "expressing support or sympathy" for an unlawful society or organization.

Some human rights and civil society organizations had difficulty obtaining government recognition as NGOs. As a result some NGOs registered as companies, which presented legal and bureaucratic obstacles to raising money to support their activities. Authorities frequently cited a lack of registration as grounds to take action against organizations. Some NGOs also reported the government monitored their activities.

c. Freedom of Religion

See the Department of State's *International Religious Freedom Report* at www.state.gov/religiousfreedomreport/.

d. Freedom of Movement, Internally Displaced Persons, Protection of Refugees, and Stateless Persons

The constitution provides for freedom of internal movement, foreign travel, emigration, and repatriation, and the government generally respected these rights. There were some restrictions, however, with respect to the eastern states of Sabah and Sarawak in particular.

Abuse of Migrants, Refugees, and Stateless Persons: The government generally did not impede organizations providing protection and assistance to internally displaced persons, refugees, returning refugees, asylum seekers, stateless persons, and other persons of concern. Access to those in detention centers, however, was often significantly delayed. Government cooperation with UNHCR and the International Organization for Migration was inconsistent, and there were several flashpoints.

In February police conducted a multiday operation checking for undocumented migrants in front of UNHCR offices in Kuala Lumpur and detained or arrested dozens entering and exiting the building. In July, UNHCR temporarily halted operations in response to a government directive barring UNHCR from issuing refugee cards to "walk-in" applicants. In mid-August, UNHCR reported its operations had returned to normal.

NGOs and international organizations involved with migrant workers, refugees, and asylum seekers made credible allegations of overcrowding, inadequate food and clothing, lack of regular access to clean water, poor medical care, improper sanitation, and lack of bedding. An NGO with access to the detention centers claimed these conditions and lack of medical screening and treatment facilitated the spread of disease and contributed to deaths. NGOs provided most of the medical care and treatment in the detention centers.

In-country Movement: Consistent with the 1963 agreement that incorporated Sabah and Sarawak into the country, these eastern states controlled immigration into their areas and required citizens from peninsular Malaysia and foreigners to present passports or national identity cards for entry. Authorities continued to deny entry to selected national opposition leaders to East Malaysian states.

Foreign Travel: Travel to Israel is subject to approval and limited to religious purposes. The government also sometimes used its powers to restrict travel by its critics. In May immigration authorities prevented Bersih Chair Maria Chin Abdullah from boarding a flight to Seoul, Korea, to accept a human rights award. Government officials did not explain the decision but noted travel abroad by citizens was a privilege not a right.

Protection of Refugees

Access to Asylum: The laws do not provide for the granting of asylum or refugee status; nonetheless, the government generally cooperated with UNHCR and occasionally reported potential persons of concern to UNHCR.

According to UNHCR there were 150,669 persons of concern, including 135,475 of Myanmar origin, as of October 31. During the year UNHCR successfully resettled 7,600 refugees.

<u>Refoulement</u>: The government did not provide legal protection against the expulsion or return of refugees to countries where their lives or freedom would be threatened based on their race, religion, nationality, membership in a particular social group, or political opinion but generally tolerated the presence of asylum seekers on its territory.

<u>Freedom of movement</u>: The government sometimes detained asylum seekers, in either police jails or immigration detention centers, until UNHCR established the asylum seekers' bona fides. Local and international NGOs estimated the population at most of the country's 17 immigration detention centers was at or beyond capacity, with some detainees held for a year or more. The number detained in these centers was not publicly available.

<u>Employment</u>: Although the government does not legally authorize UNHCR-registered refugees to work, the government typically did not interfere if they performed informal work. UNHCR reported the government brought charges, in a few cases, against employers for hiring them.

<u>Access to Basic Services</u>: For persons with UNHCR cards, the government provided access to health care for refugees at a discounted foreigner's rate but not to asylum seekers. NGOs operated mobile clinics, but access was limited. Refugees did not have access to the public education system. Access to education was limited to schools run by NGOs and ethnic communities, and UNHCR estimated no more than 30 percent of refugee children attended school. A lack of resources and qualified teachers limited opportunities for the majority of school-age refugee children. UNHCR staff members conducted numerous visits to prisons and immigration detention centers to provide counseling, support, and legal representation for refugees and asylum seekers.

<u>Temporary Protection</u>: In November the government announced plans to allow another 500 Syrian refugees to enter the country, in addition to the 78 already here. The announcement was in line with a 2015 pledge to provide temporary asylum to 3,000 such refugees over a three-year period.

Stateless Persons

UNHCR estimated there were 11,689 stateless persons in the country, 40 percent of whom were children. National Registration Department officials stated they do not keep records of stateless persons.

A number of local NGOs and SUHAKAM did research, conducted workshops, and ran public awareness campaigns on the problem of stateless children.

Foreigners may qualify for permanent resident status after several years of marriage to a citizen: five years of marriage for foreign women married to citizen men; 10 years for foreign men married to citizen women. After two years of permanent resident status, they are eligible to apply for citizenship. While awaiting permanent resident status, authorities usually granted visas to foreign spouses of citizens to allow them an extended legal stay in the country. A local advocacy group for migrant workers reported that in the last five or six years, procedures improved to include shorter waiting times in the processing of permanent residency petitions and visas. Although nationality laws in the country were not overtly discriminatory due to ethnicity or religion, there was a perception Muslims received preference.

Authorities considered children born out of wedlock to foreign women to have inherited their mother's citizenship. Authorities allow registration of such births only if the mother produces proof of her citizenship, creating a risk of statelessness because many foreign women were unable to produce a passport or other evidence. According to UNHCR, refugees or asylum seekers often did not have valid proof of citizenship. In such cases authorities entered the child's citizenship as "unknown" on the birth certificate. UNHCR deemed this a widespread problem and reported in November there was a population of approximately 80,000 Filipino Muslim refugees in the eastern state of Sabah. Of these an estimated 10,000 were children without birth documentation and thus technically stateless.

Although children born in the country of illegal migrant mothers married to citizen men are eligible for citizenship, the mother may have difficulty registering the marriage and subsequently the child's citizenship because of inability to provide a valid passport or identification document. Some observers indicated that children born to Muslim refugees and asylum seekers often had an easier time obtaining citizenship than non-Muslim refugees and asylum seekers. For refugees in Muslim marriages, the observers claimed authorities often accepted a UNHCR document or other documentation in lieu of a passport.

Persons who lacked proof of citizenship were not able to attend school, access government services such as reduced cost health care, or own property. UNHCR may provide birth registration or other documentation in some cases.

By law authorities consider illegal anyone entering the country without appropriate documentation. Such persons face a mandatory maximum five years' imprisonment, a maximum fine of 10,000 RM ($2,250), or both, and mandatory caning of not more than six strokes.

Section 3. Freedom to Participate in the Political Process

The law provides citizens the ability to choose their government through free and fair elections held by secret ballot and based on universal and equal suffrage. Nonetheless, opposition political parties were disadvantaged due to government control over traditional media outlets and the Election Commission that oversees voter registration and constituency boundaries. The ruling government coalition has not changed since 1957. While authorities generally recorded votes accurately, there were irregularities that affected the fairness of elections. The constitution does not recognize differences in the population size of electoral constituencies of each district, and each constituency, regardless of population size, is represented by one parliamentary seat. The number of inhabitants in electoral districts varies, with rural districts generally smaller in population than urban districts. For example, the rural district of Igan had 18,000 registered voters with one representative, while the urban district of Kapar had more than 144,000 registered voters with one representative. This regulation has the effect of strongly overrepresenting the rural vote, which the constitution mandates as part of the agreement for the states of Sabah and Sarawak to join the federation in 1963. Voters do not elect local and municipal leaders, who are appointed at the state or federal level.

Elections and Political Participation

Recent Elections: Following two parliamentary by-elections in June, opposition parties and NGOs accused the Election Commission of moving the names of more than 100,000 voters throughout the country to neighboring constituencies without informing the voters or obtaining parliamentary approval for the changes. Critics of the Election Commission called the action unconstitutional and "sleight-of-hand" gerrymandering, which affected some voters in the by-elections. Election Commission officials claimed the transfers moved voters to closer poll centers, easing the voting process.

In May the Sarawak State government, which maintains autonomy over immigration, barred entry to key opposition leaders from other states during the state election campaign.

The overrepresentation of some constituencies affected national elections in 2013, when the ruling coalition won 133 of 222 seats, with many of its victories coming in more heavily weighted rural areas. Opposition parties won 52 percent of the popular vote but failed to gain a majority in parliament. In a post-election report, electoral reform coalition Bersih cited the lack of independence of the Election Commission, which reports directly to the prime minister, as an unfair advantage to the ruling BN.

<u>Political Parties and Political Participation</u>: Opposition parties were unable to compete on equal terms with the UMNO-led BN coalition and were subject to restrictions and outside interference. The lack of equal access to media was a serious problem for the opposition in national elections. News about the opposition was restricted and reported in a biased fashion in print and broadcast media. Registering a new political party remained difficult because of government restrictions on the process.

<u>Participation of Women and Minorities</u>: Women faced no legal limits on participation in government and politics, but they occupied few senior roles.

The politically dominant Malay ethnic majority held the most powerful government senior leadership positions. Non-Malays filled 12 of the 36 ministerial posts and 11 of the 32 deputy minister positions. There were only three female ministers and five female deputy ministers.

Section 4. Corruption and Lack of Transparency in Government

The law provides criminal penalties for official corruption; however, enforcement generally focused on relatively small-scale, low-level crime. There was a broadly held perception of widespread corruption and cronyism within the ruling coalition and in government institutions. Media reported numerous cases of alleged official corruption.

<u>Corruption</u>: While the government successfully prosecuted some bribe-taking officials and persons paying bribes, observers noted the government neither prosecuted nor convicted many senior officials. Journalists, activists, and

politicians were harassed and prosecuted after publicly reporting on or criticizing senior-level corruption.

The Malaysian Anti-Corruption Commission (MACC) is responsible for investigating and prosecuting corruption of both private and public bodies. An auditor general has the responsibility, set forth in the constitution, to audit the accounts of the federal and state governments, government agencies, and other public authorities. Media reports and statements by civil society and opposition leaders questioned the government's ability to prosecute corruption of high-ranking government officials.

In August the top three MACC officials retired or transferred to other ministries. Opposition leaders and NGOs criticized the changes as "the death knell of the MACC" following multiple transfers of other key personnel in 2015 that stalled investigations into billions of dollars in funds allegedly stolen from state-owned development company 1MDB. The MACC's new leadership, however, publicized several high-profile cases during the year and arrested high-ranking officials from both the private and public sectors. In September the anticorruption body charged a high-ranking Kuala Lumpur city official over a graft scheme involving 4.5 million RM ($1.01 million). On September 7, MACC authorities charged Abdul Aziz Zainal, the chair of national Bank Rakyat, for abetting the theft of almost 15 million RM ($3.37 million) from the institution.

Financial Disclosure: Cabinet members must declare their assets to the prime minister. Senior civil servants are required to declare their assets to the chief secretary of the government. Junior civil servants must declare their assets to the head of their department. The assets, liabilities, and interests public officials must declare are clearly defined and do not include the assets and incomes of spouses and dependent children. Public officials must declare their assets annually and not upon entry or exit of their posting. Those who refuse or fail to declare their assets face disciplinary actions and are ineligible for promotion. The government did not make public these declarations.

Public Access to Information: The law prohibits dissemination of a wide variety of documents classified by a minister in the federal government, a chief minister of a state, or similar public officers. Critics accused the government of using these powers to prevent dissemination of materials and stifle dissent. Members of parliament may obtain information protected by government classification on an individual basis, and some then made it available to the public.

The states of Selangor and Penang, both controlled by the opposition coalition, are the only states with freedom of information laws that allow public access to certain state documents.

Section 5. Governmental Attitude Regarding International and Nongovernmental Investigation of Alleged Violations of Human Rights

A number of domestic and international human rights groups generally operated without government restriction, investigating and publishing their findings on human rights cases. Government officials were cooperative and responsive to their views.

The government generally allowed NGOs to function independently, met with representatives from some NGOs, and responded to some NGO requests. The government, however, also took actions against some NGOs.

Government Human Rights Bodies: Created by an act of parliament, the official human rights commission SUHAKAM is headed by a chairperson and commissioners appointed by the king on the recommendation of the prime minister. Observers generally considered SUHAKAM a credible human rights monitor. It conducted training, undertook investigations, provided reports, and made recommendations to the government. SUHAKAM is not empowered to inquire into allegations relating to court cases in progress and must cease an inquiry if an allegation under investigation becomes the subject of a court case. Due to a 50 percent government reduction to its annual budget, SUHAKAM reduced the scope of its work during the year and continued to seek alternative sources of funding.

Section 6. Discrimination, Societal Abuses, and Trafficking in Persons

Women

Rape and Domestic Violence: Rape, including marital rape, is a criminal offense, as are most forms of domestic violence. Rape is punishable by a maximum 20 years' imprisonment and caning. Marital rape does not have a minimum penalty, but the maximum penalty is five years' imprisonment. According to women's groups, on average 10 women in the country were raped each day; more than half of these women were younger than 16 years. According to the latest statistics from the Ministry of Home Affairs, 28,741 rape cases were reported from 2005 to 2014 with 16 percent (4,514 cases) taken to court and 2.7 percent (765 cases) with guilty verdicts. According to police statistics, in 2014 there were 4,807 reported cases of domestic violence, 2,045 cases of rape, and 1,590 cases of sexual harassment.

Cultural attitudes and a reported lack of sympathy from the largely male police force resulted in many victims not reporting rapes. Many government hospitals had crisis centers where victims of rape and domestic abuse could make reports without going to a police station. NGOs and political parties also cooperated to provide counseling for rape victims. Women's groups asserted the courts were inconsistent in punishing rapists.

Although the government, NGOs, and political parties maintained shelters and offered other assistance to battered spouses, activists asserted that support mechanisms for victims of domestic violence remained inadequate. There is a sexual investigations unit at each police headquarters to help victims of sexual crimes and abuse. Moreover police sometimes assign psychologists or counselors to provide emotional support. Women's rights activists reported that police needed additional training in handling domestic abuse and rape cases. Reports of rape and spousal abuse drew considerable government, NGO, and press attention.

Female Genital Mutilation/Cutting (FGM/C): Ministry of Health guidelines allow the common practice but only at government health-care facilities. A 2012 university study on FGM/C--the latest information available--reported more than 90 percent of the Muslim women respondents had undergone FGM/C. The most common reasons cited for its practice were religious obligation, hygienic purposes, and cultural tradition. In 2009 the Fatwa Committee of the National Council of Islamic Religious Affairs ruled "female circumcision" obligatory for Muslims but "if found to be harmful to health must be avoided."

Sexual Harassment: The law prohibits a person in authority from using his position to intimidate a subordinate to have sexual relations. The law classifies some types of workplace sexual harassment as criminal offenses (see section 7.d.). A government voluntary code of conduct provides a detailed definition of sexual harassment intended to raise public awareness of the problem. Observers noted that authorities took claims seriously, but victims were often reluctant to report sexual harassment because of embarrassment, the difficulty of proving the offense, and a lengthy trial process.

Reproductive Rights: Couples and individuals have the right to decide the number, spacing, and timing of their children; manage their reproductive health; and have access to the information and means to do so, free from discrimination, coercion, or violence. Authorities permitted access to contraceptives, and they were locally available. The UN Population Fund estimated use of modern contraceptives by women of reproductive age was 42 percent and the unmet demand for family planning was 15 percent. Skilled medical personnel attended 99 percent of births, and women generally had access to postpartum care. Local and international NGOs confirmed that hospitals prevented refugee mothers from removing their newborn children from the hospital until they paid the hospital bill.

Discrimination: The constitution prohibits discrimination against citizens based on gender. The law allows polygyny for Muslims, which a small minority of men practiced. Islamic inheritance law generally favors male offspring and male relatives. While sharia generally requires a husband's consent for divorce, a small but steadily increasing number of women were able to obtain divorces under sharia without their husband's consent. Non-Muslim women are subject to civil and criminal law but not sharia. The constitution gives men and women equal rights to inherit, acquire, own, manage, or dispose of any property, including land. Civil law gives non-Muslim mothers and fathers equal parental rights, while sharia favors fathers. Four states--Johor, Selangor, Negri Sembilan, and Pahang--extend equal parental rights to Muslim mothers, and women's groups continued to urge the other states to do the same.

The law requires equal pay for male and female workers for work of equal value. Nonetheless, NGOs reported continued discrimination against women in the workplace in terms of promotion and salary (see section 7.d.).

Children

Birth Registration: The constitution stipulates that a child born in the country can be granted nationality only if one parent is a citizen or permanent resident at the time of birth. The law does not grant citizenship automatically, and parents must register a child within 14 days of birth. Authorities require citizens to provide their marriage certificate and both parents' government identity cards. Noncitizens must provide a passport. Parents applying for late registration must provide proof the child was born in the country. Authorities do not enter the father's information for a child born out of wedlock unless there is a joint application by both parents. Authorities do not register children born to illegal immigrants or asylum seekers. UNHCR registered children born to refugees.

Education: Education is free, compulsory, and universal through primary school (six years). Although primary education is compulsory, there was no enforcement mechanism governing school attendance.

The UN Children's Fund's *State of the World's Children 2014* report highlighted secondary school enrollment as a cause for concern. Secondary school enrollment comprised 71 percent of girls and 66 percent of boys, compared with 96 percent overall enrollment in primary school.

Child Abuse: Child abuse took the form of neglect (failure to provide basic needs), physical abuse, sexual abuse, and infant abandonment. Punishment for child abuse includes fines, imprisonment, caning, or a combination of these measures. According to SUHAKAM the government filed 2,189 charges of child sexual abuse with only 140 successful convictions from January 2012 to July.

The government focused on preventing sexual exploitation of children, including commercial sexual exploitation. Incest also was a problem. The law provides for six to 20 years' imprisonment and caning for individuals convicted of incest. A child's testimony is acceptable only if there is corroborating evidence. This posed special problems for molestation cases in which the child victim was the only witness.

Early and Forced Marriage: The minimum age of marriage is 18 years for men and 16 years for women. Muslim women younger than 16 years may marry with the approval of a sharia court. The country's Sharia Judiciary Department reported 10,270 child marriage applications from 2005 to 2015. In some cases authorities treated early marriage as a solution to statutory rape. In June a court in Sarawak State acquitted a man of statutory rape after he married the 14-year-old victim. The government prosecutor was appealing the decision. In October the Ministry of Women, Family, and Community Development reported it had set up a task force to help regulate early marriages and limit abuses.

Sexual Exploitation of Children: A conviction for trafficking in persons involving a child for the purposes of sexual exploitation carries a punishment of three to 20 years' imprisonment and a fine. Under the law the minimum age for consensual, noncommercial sex is 16 years for both boys and girls. Homosexual acts are illegal regardless of age or consent. Sharia forbids sex outside of wedlock regardless of age or consent.

The law outlaws pornography and states that a child is considered a victim of sexual abuse if he or she has taken part, whether as a participant or an observer, in any activity that is sexual in nature for the purposes of a photograph, recording, film, videotape, or performance. Child prostitution existed, but authorities often treated children in prostitution as offenders or undocumented immigrants rather than as victims.

Displaced Children: The prevalence of street children was a problem in Sabah. Estimates of the street children population ranged from a few hundred to 15,000, many of whom were born in the country to illegal immigrant parents. Authorities deported some of these parents, leaving the children without guardians. These unaccompanied children lacked citizenship and access to schooling or other government-provided support and often resorted to menial labor, criminal activities, and prostitution to survive; those living on the streets were vulnerable to forced labor, including forced begging.

International Child Abductions: The country is not a party to the 1980 Hague Convention on the Civil Aspects of International Child Abduction. See the Department of State's *Annual Report on International Parental Child Abduction* at travel.state.gov/content/childabduction/en/legal/compliance.html.

Anti-Semitism

The country's Jewish population was estimated to be between 100 and 200 persons. Anti-Semitism was a serious problem across the political spectrum and attracted wide support among segments of the population. A 2015 Anti-Defamation League survey found 61 percent of citizens held anti-Jewish attitudes. Government-owned newspapers and statements by current and former political officeholders sometimes blamed civil society activity on "Jewish plots" or "Jewish conspiracies."

In March Deputy Minister of Agriculture Tajuddin Abdul Rahman, a leader of the ruling UMNO party, accused government critics of working with "media controlled by Jews" to bring down PM Najib.

Trafficking in Persons

See the Department of State's *Trafficking in Persons Report* at www.state.gov/j/tip/rls/tiprpt/.

Persons with Disabilities

The law gives persons with disabilities the right to equal access and use of public facilities, amenities, services, and buildings open or provided to the public. The Ministry of Women, Family, and Community Development is responsible for safeguarding the rights of persons with disabilities.

New government buildings generally had a full range of facilities for persons with disabilities. The government, however, did not mandate accessibility to transportation for persons with disabilities, and authorities retrofitted few older public facilities to provide access to persons with disabilities. Recognizing public transportation was not "disabled-friendly," the government maintained its 50 percent reduction of excise duty on locally made cars and motorcycles adapted for persons with disabilities.

Employment discrimination occurred in relation to persons with disabilities (see section 7.d.). Students with disabilities attended mainstream schools, but accessibility remained a serious problem. Separate education facilities also existed, but were insufficient to meet the needs of all students with disabilities.

National/Racial/Ethnic Minorities

The constitution gives ethnic Malays and other indigenous groups, collectively known as "bumiputra," a "special position" in the country, a status not accorded to ethnic Chinese or Indians. Government regulations and policies provide for extensive preferential programs designed to boost the economic position of bumiputra, who constitute a majority of the population. Such programs limited opportunities for non-bumiputra in higher education and government employment. Many industries were subject to race-based requirements that mandated bumiputra ownership levels; government procurement and licensing policies favor bumiputra-owned businesses. According to the government, these policies were necessary to attain ethnic harmony and political stability.

Despite the government's stated goal of poverty alleviation, these race-based policies were not subject to upper-income limitations and contributed to widening economic disparity within the bumiputra community. Ethnic Indian citizens, who similarly to ethnic Chinese citizens do not receive such privileges, remained among the country's poorest groups.

Indigenous People

The constitution provides indigenous and nonindigenous people with the same civil and political rights, but the government did not effectively protect these rights. NGOs reported authorities frequently ignored indigenous people's efforts to obtain identity cards.

Indigenous people in peninsular Malaysia, known as Orang Asli, had very little ability to participate in decisions that affected them. A constitutional provision provides for "the special position of the Malays and natives of any of the States of Sabah and Sarawak," but it does not refer specifically to the Orang Asli. This ambiguity over the community's status in the constitution led to selective interpretation by different public institutions. For example, although several states designated land for Orang Asli communities, an NGO claimed the national land code (which provides permanency of tenure to the more generous-sized lands of the indigenous peoples of Sabah and Sarawak) does not cover these lands.

The Orang Asli, who numbered approximately 180,000 (0.86 percent of the population) constituted the poorest group in the country. They do not own the land they live on, but rather the government permits them to live on designated land as at-will tenants, typically without documentation. The government can seize this land if it provides compensation. There were confrontations between the Orang Asli and logging companies over land disputes, and the uncertainty over their land tenure made the Orang Asli vulnerable to exploitation.

Indigenous people in Sabah and Sarawak protested encroachment by state and private logging and plantation companies onto land they considered theirs under native customary rights. They were disadvantaged, however, by laws allowing purchase of land with perfunctory newspaper notifications, to which indigenous persons might not have access. Indigenous groups also reported harassment by logging companies.

The Sarawak State government's plan to build 12 hydroelectric dams threatened to displace tens of thousands of indigenous peoples.

Human rights organizations argued the June 21 murder of opposition politician Bill Kayong was motivated by the politician's activism on land rights issues. Authorities arrested several suspects over the murder but prosecutors have not revealed a motive for the crime.

Acts of Violence, Discrimination, and Other Abuses Based on Sexual Orientation and Gender Identity

The law states that sodomy and oral sex acts are "carnal intercourse against the order of nature," but authorities rarely enforced it. It was, however, the basis for the controversial case against parliamentary opposition leader Anwar Ibrahim (see section 1.e.), currently serving a five-year prison sentence. Religious and cultural taboos against same-sex sexual conduct were widespread (see section 2.a.).

Authorities often charged transgender individuals for "indecent behavior" and "importuning for immoral purposes" in public. Those convicted of a first offense faced a maximum fine of 25 RM ($5.60) and a maximum sentence of 14 days in jail. The sentences for subsequent convictions may be maximum fines of 100 RM ($22.50) and a maximum of three months in jail. Local advocates contended that those imprisoned served their time in the male prison population where police and inmates often abused them verbally and sexually.

In April a gay student sought and gained refugee status in Canada after a local news site published his story along with a poll encouraging violence against the student.

Section 7. Worker Rights

a. Freedom of Association and the Right to Collective Bargaining

The law provides for limited freedom of association and for some categories of workers to form and join trade unions, subject to a variety of legal and practical restrictions. The law provides for the right to strike and to bargain collectively, but both were severely restricted. The law prohibits employers from interfering with union activities, including union formation. It prohibits employers from seeking retribution for legal union activities and requires reinstatement of workers fired for union activity.

The law prohibits defense and police officials, retired or dismissed workers, or workers categorized as "confidential, managerial, and executive" from joining a union. The law also restricts the formation of unions to workers in "similar" trades, occupations, or industries. Foreign workers may join a trade union but cannot hold union office, unless they obtain permission from the Ministry of Human Resources. In view of the absence of a direct employment relationship with owners of a workplace, contract workers may not form a union and cannot negotiate or benefit from collective bargaining agreements.

The director general of trade unions and the minister of human resources may refuse to register or withdraw registration from some unions without judicial oversight. Authorities consider a trade union an unlawful association if the union's registration was refused, withdrawn, or canceled. Trade unions may affiliate with international trade union organizations, subject to the approval of the director general of trade unions.

Most private-sector workers have the right to bargain collectively, although these negotiations cannot include issues of transfer, promotion, appointments, dismissal, and reinstatement. The law restricts collective bargaining in "pioneer" industries the government has identified as growth priorities, including various high tech fields. Public-sector workers have some collective bargaining rights, although some could only express opinions on wages and working conditions instead of actively negotiating. If a union initiates collective bargaining, employers are not mandated to accept the invitation. If negotiations stall or an employer refuses to negotiate, the union may appeal to the director general of trade unions to conciliate. If the parties are still unable to agree, the Ministry of Human Resources may refer the dispute to the Industrial Court for binding arbitration.

Private-sector strikes are legal, although they were severely restricted. The law provides for penal sanctions for peaceful strikes. Union officials claimed legal requirements for strikes were almost impossible to meet. The law prohibits general strikes, and trade unions may not strike over disputes related to trade union registration or illegal dismissals. Workers may not strike in a broad range of industries deemed "essential," nor may they hold strikes when a dispute is before the Industrial Court.

The government did not effectively enforce laws prohibiting employers from seeking retribution for legal union activities and requiring reinstatement of workers fired for trade union activity. Penalties for violations include a fine of up to 10,000 RM ($2,250) but were seldom assessed and generally not sufficient to deter violations. There continued to be long delays in the treatment of union claims to obtain recognition for collective bargaining purposes. In March, however, a court found an electronics company guilty of union busting for the company's 2010 and 2011 conduct retaliating against an employee advocating the establishment of a regional union for the electronic industry. In September the court ordered the company to recognize the union, but it did not issue a penalty.

Freedom of association and collective bargaining were not fully respected. While the Ministry of Labor prohibits national-level unions, it allows three regional territorial federations of unions (Peninsular Malaysia, Sabah, and Sarawak) to operate. They exercised many of the responsibilities of national-level labor unions, although they could not bargain on behalf of local unions. The Malaysian Trade Unions Congress (MTUC) is a registered "society" of trade unions in both the private and government sectors that does not have the right to bargain collectively or strike but may provide technical support to affiliated members. Some workers' organizations were independent of government, political parties, and employers, but employer-dominated or "yellow" unions were reportedly a concern.

The inability of unions to provide more than limited protection for workers, particularly foreign workers who continued to face threat of deportation, and the prevalence of antiunion discrimination created a disincentive to unionize. In some instances companies reportedly harassed leaders of unions that sought recognition. Some trade unions reported the government detained or restricted the movement of some union members under laws allowing temporary detention without charging the detainee with a crime. Trade unions asserted some workers had wages withheld or were terminated because of union-related activity. A terminated worker legally ceases to be a member of his or her trade union. Labor activists noted that the loss of membership upon termination comes when trade union support and assistance is most necessary.

The time needed for a union to be recognized remained unpredictable and long. Union officials expressed frustration about delays in the settlement of union recognition disputes; such applications were often refused. If a union's recognition request was approved, the employer sometimes challenged the decision in court, leading to multi-year delays in recognizing unions.

b. Prohibition of Forced or Compulsory Labor

The law prohibits all forms of forced or compulsory labor. Five agencies, including the Department of Labor, have enforcement powers under the law, but their officers did not always actively search for indications of forced labor. NGOs continued to criticize the lack of resources dedicated to the enforcement of the law. The government continued efforts to enforce laws prohibiting forced labor. In August the government secured Thailand's approval to extradite 10 suspects alleged to have trafficked Rohingya and other groups, whose remains were found in mass graves on both sides of the Malaysia-Thailand border in 2015. As of October no local perpetrators were convicted in connection with these investigations.

The labor department relied on evidence of three months' nonpayment of wages in order to initiate an investigation into a potential forced labor case. Potential penalties included maximum fines of 10,000 RM ($2,250). In addition to these fines, authorities often charged forced labor perpetrators with connected crimes that included harsher penalties. For example, the anti-human trafficking law allows a maximum 20 years' imprisonment and a fine, depending on the nature of the offense.

In May the government adopted regulations to implement the 2015 amendments to its anti-trafficking legislation, which, if fully implemented, would allow trafficking victims to move freely and work; give broader access by NGOs to provide protection to trafficking victims; and establish a high-level government committee to advance trafficking-related initiatives.

The national anti-human trafficking council reported that Department of Labor officials received specialized training, including with other law enforcement agencies, to help increase coordination. In the labor department, there were 30 to 40 "special enforcement officers" who focused primarily on forced labor and other human trafficking indicators. These officers, however, also performed a variety of functions and were responsible for inspections, investigation of complaints, workplace assessments, adjudication of disputes, and consultations with companies regarding compliance (see section 7.e.). Authorities investigated most cases of wage withholding as violations of the Employment Act, rather than of the Anti-trafficking in Persons and Anti-Smuggling of Migrants Act. In cases where inspectors found indicators of possible human trafficking (e.g., physical abuse, mental abuse, or worker confinement), inspectors referred these cases as human trafficking and collaborated with police and the Ministry of Home Affairs.

Forced labor occurred in the country. A variety of sources reported occurrences of forced labor, or conditions indicative of forced labor, in plantation agriculture, the fishing industry, electronics factories, garment production, construction, restaurants, and domestic households, among adults and children (also see section 7.c).

Employers, employment agents, or labor recruiters subjected some migrants to forced labor or debt bondage. Labor activists and human rights NGOs reported debt bondage often characterized conditions for migrant workers on some plantations as well as in some factories and other businesses. Many companies hired foreign workers using recruiting or outsourcing companies rather than directly by the factory or plantation where they worked, creating uncertainty regarding the legal relationship between the worker and the outsourcing company or owner of the workplace, and making workers more vulnerable to exploitation and complicating dispute resolution. Labor union representatives described a typical pattern involving recruiting agents both in the countries of origin and in the country who imposed high fees, which made migrant workers vulnerable to debt bondage.

Passport confiscation by employers of migrant workers, which was widespread and generally went unpunished, increased workers' vulnerability to forced labor. Migrant workers without access to their passports were more vulnerable to harsh working conditions, lower wages than promised, unexpected wage deductions, and poor housing. NGOs reported that agents or employers in some cases drafted contracts including a provision for employees to sign over the right to hold their passports to the employer or an agent. Some employers and migrant workers reported that workers sometimes requested the employer to keep their passports, since replacing lost or stolen passports could cost several months' wages and leave foreign workers open to questions about their legal status.

Also see the Department of State's *Trafficking in Persons Report* at www.state.gov/j/tip/rls/tiprpt/.

c. Prohibition of Child Labor and Minimum Age for Employment

The law prohibits the employment of children younger than 14 years but permits some exceptions, such as light work in a family enterprise, work in public entertainment, work performed for the government in a school or in training institutions, or work as an approved apprentice. There is no minimum age for engaging in light work. In no case may a child work more than six hours per day, more than six days per week, or at night. For children between 14 and 18 years, there was no list clarifying specific occupations or sectors considered hazardous and therefore prohibited.

The government maintained that migrant workers had largely replaced child labor and that it vigorously enforced child labor provisions. Those found contravening child labor laws faced a maximum imprisonment of six months, a maximum fine of 2,000 RM ($450), or both. Violators in subsequent offenses faced punishment of a maximum two years' imprisonment, a maximum fine of 3,000 RM ($675), or both.

Child labor occurred in some family businesses. Child labor in urban areas was common in the informal sector, including family food businesses and night markets, and in small-scale industry. Child labor was also evident among migrant

domestic workers. There was no comprehensive data available on the occurrence
of child labor. The International Labor Organization encouraged the government
to take steps to make such data available.

NGOs reported that stateless children in Sabah were especially vulnerable to labor
exploitation in palm oil production, forced begging, and work in service industries,
including restaurants. Although the National Union of Plantation Workers
reported it was rare to find children involved in plantation work in peninsular
Malaysia, others reported instances of child labor on palm oil plantations across the
country. Commercial sexual exploitation of children, a worst form of child labor,
also occurred (see section 6, Children).

d. Discrimination with Respect to Employment and Occupation

The law does not prohibit discrimination with respect to hiring, although the
director general of labor may investigate discrimination in the terms and conditions
of employment for both foreign and local employees. The director general may
issue to the employer directives necessary to resolve the matter. Failure to comply
could result in a fine of not more than 10,000 RM ($2,250).

Employers are obligated to inquire into most sexual harassment complaints in a
prescribed manner. The penalty for noncompliance is a maximum fine of 10,000
RM ($2,250). Advocacy groups such as the Association of Women Lawyers stated
these provisions were not comprehensive enough to provide adequate help to
victims.

Migrant workers must undergo mandatory testing for more than 16 illnesses (as
well as pregnancy). Employers may immediately deport pregnant or ill workers.
A regulation reserves 1 percent of public-sector jobs for persons with disabilities.
The law prohibits women from engaging in "underground working" and restricts
employers from requiring female employees to work in industrial or agricultural
work between 10 p.m. and 5 a.m. or to commence work for the day without having
11 consecutive hours of rest since the end of the last work period.

Discrimination in employment and occupation occurred with respect to women;
members of national, racial, and ethnic minorities; and persons with disabilities. A
code of practice guides all government agencies, employers, employee
associations, employees, and others with respect to placement of persons with
disabilities in private sector jobs. Disability rights NGOs reported employers were
reluctant to hire individuals with disabilities.

The government reserved large quotas for the bumiputra majority regarding positions in the federal civil service and regarding vocational permits and licenses in a wide range of industries, which greatly reduced economic opportunity for minority groups (see section 6).

Women experienced some economic discrimination in access to employment. A UN report noted participation in the labor market for women was 46.1 percent, compared to 78.7 percent for men. Employers routinely asked women their marital status during job interviews. The Association of Women Lawyers advocated for passage of a separate sexual harassment bill making it compulsory for employers to formulate sexual harassment policies.

Migrant workers also faced employment discrimination (see sections 7.b. and 7.e.). Employers were also unilaterally able to terminate work permits, subjecting migrant workers to immediate deportation.

e. Acceptable Conditions of Work

The minimum wage was 920 RM ($205) per month in the states of Sabah and Sarawak and 1,000 RM ($225) per month in peninsular Malaysia. The minimum wage applied to both citizen and foreign workers in most sectors, with the exception of domestic service (see below). The minimum wage rates were less than the Ministry of Finance-published poverty income levels in Sabah and Sarawak.

Working hours may not exceed eight hours per day or 48 hours per week, unless workers receive overtime pay. Each workweek must include a 24-hour rest period. The law also sets overtime rates of 1.5 times the base hourly rate for regular overtime, two times the regular hourly rate for work on rest days, and three times the regular hourly rate for work on the 10 mandated public holidays. It mandates public holidays, annual leave, sick leave, and maternity allowances. The law specifies limits on overtime, which vary by sector, but it allows for exceptions.

The law provides for protections for foreign domestic workers only with regard to wages and contract termination. The law excludes them from provisions that would otherwise stipulate one rest day per week, an eight-hour workday, and a 48-hour workweek. Instead, bilateral agreements or memoranda of understanding between the government and some countries of migrant workers' origin include provisions for rest periods, compensation, and other conditions of employment for migrant domestic workers, including prohibitions on passport retention.

Occupational health and safety laws cover all sectors of the economy except the maritime sector and the armed forces. The law requires workers to use safety equipment and cooperate with employers to create a safe, healthy workplace, but it does not specify a right to remove oneself from a hazardous or dangerous situation without penalty. Laws on worker's compensation cover both local and migrant workers but provide no protection for migrant domestic workers.

The National Wages Consultative Council is responsible for recommending changes to the minimum wage and coverage for various sectors, types of employment, and regions. The labor department of the Ministry of Human Resources is responsible for enforcing standards on wages, working conditions, and occupational safety and health. There were approximately 500 labor enforcement officers for the country. These officials were responsible for enforcing labor law at hundreds of thousands of businesses and in private residences that employ domestic help. Labor department officials reported they sought to conduct labor inspections as frequently as possible. Nevertheless, many businesses could operate for years without an inspection. Inspections occurred both as scheduled events and surprise visits.

The national Occupational Safety and Health Council--composed of workers, employers, and government representatives--creates and coordinates implementation of occupational health and safety measures. It requires employers to identify risks and take precautions, including providing safety training to workers, and compels companies with more than 40 workers to establish joint management-employee safety committees.

Penalties for employers who fail to follow the law begin with a maximum fine of 10,000 RM ($2,250) per employee and can rise to a maximum five years' imprisonment. Employers can be required to pay back wages plus the fine. If they refuse to comply, employers face additional fines of 100,000 RM ($22,500) per day that wages are not paid. Employers or employees who violate occupational health and safety laws are subject to maximum fines of 50,000 RM ($11,250), maximum two years' imprisonment, or both. The government attempted to inform workers of their rights, encouraged workers to come forward with their complaints, and warned employers to end abuses.

Workers have the right to take legal action against abusive employers. NGOs reported courts generally sided with employees and ruled employers must pay back salaries and compensate plaintiffs for injuries. Nonetheless, NGOs claimed some labor contractors regularly used intimidation tactics and physical abuse to prevent exploited workers from seeking justice. In 2015 the government amended the law to enhance the protection of victims, but it was still finalizing the details of implementation as of November. Mechanisms for monitoring workplace conditions were inadequate. Private, for-profit labor contractors, themselves often guilty of abuses, were often responsible for the resolution of abuse cases. Labor enforcement officers investigated and adjudicated many violations of labor law and did not refer them to labor court or pursue them as criminal cases. Labor officers have authority to mediate and resolve disputes involving minor violations discovered during routine inspections. Many employees reportedly agreed to such mediation since they viewed it as the most expedient way to recoup owed wages or resolve other minor issues. Mechanisms to ensure good conditions for domestic workers in private residences did not exist.

Employers did not respect laws on wages and working hours. The MTUC reported that 12-, 14-, and 18-hour days were common in food and other service industries. In general migrant workers were more apt to face poor working conditions, worked in sectors where violations were common, and faced challenges in accessing justice. Migrant workers, documented and undocumented, often worked under difficult conditions, performed hazardous duties, had their pay withheld by employers, and had no meaningful access to legal counsel in cases of contract violations and abuse. Some workers alleged their employers subjected them to inhuman living conditions, confiscated their travel documents, and physically assaulted them. Employers of domestic workers sometimes failed to honor the terms of employment and subjected workers to abuse. Employers reportedly restricted workers' movement and use of mobile telephones; provided substandard food and living conditions; physically and sexually assaulted workers; and harassed and threatened workers, including with deportation.

According to June statistics by the Department of Occupational Safety and Health, 125 workers died, 2,003 acquired a nonpermanent disability and 78 acquired permanent disability in the first half of the year.